Introduction

Acronym for Active Server Pages

They are pages that deal with the server side and are dedicated to building large sites, which are called dynamics as well as small sites alike

What are dynamic sites

Sites that have a database, send emails and record different data such as company products, bank customers, factory management, and so on all large sites.

How this technology works

For this to work must be auxiliary factors. For example, man speaks a language .. Also this technique speaks several different languages

Like C-Sharp - Visual Basic .NET

In the book, the focus is only on C-Sharp because it is the most widely spoken language in the work of more than ninety percent between the world's programmers and programming companies and others. What we are interested in is after the course. I mean to be able to work in free projects or in a company or with programmers.

Asp.net technology has an extension ie the page is the last extension or characters are .Aspx

Such as Page1.aspx

One of the business requirements is IIS, which prepares your computer to work and make it a local server so you can experience the sites you create on it. It is automatically installed with Visual Studio.

Hosting Type

Hosting is where you put your site after you make it .. It is of course on the Internet

The type of hosting that works with this technique is Windows hosting.

Chapter One

Use standard controls

This is the first lesson of the "Introduction to ASP.net" series, in which we will try to bring Microsoft's ASP.net platform to beginners, which is detailed into lessons. Each lesson talks about a specific topic. The basic controls built into the ASP.NET platform are essential for creating web applications, where we will learn how to display information using the Label and Literal tools, and how to accept and handle user income through the TextBox, CheckBox, and RadioButton tools.

View information

The ASP.NET platform supports two tools for displaying text data Label, Literal. While Literal displays data in a simple way, the Label tool offers many additional features and formats.

Use the Label control

We use the information display tools so that we can modify the text displayed on the page at the time of execution where we can simply select the text to be displayed by assigning the text property of the Label tool, we can also use html formats for this tool to interpret them and generate the desired output, and by default this tool surrounds The text with the tag <span>, in the following code we show different methods of assigning information to the Label tools:

ASP.net code

```
<div>
    <asp: Label ID = "Label1" runat = "server" Text = "Hi i'm Label1"> </ asp: Label>
    <br />
    <asp: Label ID = "Label2" runat = "server" Text = "Label">
    Hi i'm Label2
    </ asp: Label>
    <br />
    <asp: Label ID = "Label3" runat = "server" Text = "<b> <i> Hi i'm Label3 </i> </b>">
```

</ asp: Label>

</div>

The Label tool supports many text formatting features, including:

BackColor: Change the background color of the tool.

BorderColor: Sets the color of a frame that surrounds the Label tool.

BorderStyle: Specify the window style to display, this property can take one of the following values: NotSet, None, Dotted, Dashed, Solid, Double, Groove, Ridge, Inset, Outset.

BorderWidth: Specifies the thickness of the window.

CssClass: Specifies the CSS row to be applied to this tool.

Font: Specifies the type of font used.

ForeColor: Specifies the font color.

Style: Applies a specific design to the Label tool.

ToolTip: Text that is displayed as a tip when the mouse passes over the Label tool.

The Label tool is usually used to display titles for other tools to help the user do his work, so this tool has the AssociatedControlID property to identify the associated tool and it is generally recommended to use this property.

Use the Literal control

This tool works very similar to the work of the tool Label, but it does not enclose the text tag <span> This is what we may need in some sites where can not translate html code (such as determining the title of the page on the browser for example), and since this tool does not support the tag <span> It is also Its properties do not support CssClass, BackColor, Literal supports an important feature and is not supported by the Label tool, which is the Mode property, which can take one of the following three values:

PassThrough: Interpret the html symbols found in the text and display what they mean.

Encode: Displays text without translating html symbols where they appear.

Transform: Only symbols supported by the requesting device are interpreted for the page.

ASP.net code

```
<div>

    <asp: Literal ID = "L1" runat = "server" Mode =
"PassThrough" Text = "<hr />" />

    <asp: Literal ID = "L2" runat = "server" Mode =
"Encode" Text = "<hr />" />

    <asp: Literal ID = "L3" runat = "server" Mode =
"Transform" Text = "<hr />" />

</div>
```

When performing the previous page, Literal1 displays a horizontal line, Literal2 displays the text </hr>, while Literal3 scans the requesting device for the page. If it supports this tag, it displays a horizontal line or the text will be displayed as is </hr>.

Accept user income

The ASP.NET platform includes tools that allow the user to enter and make choices on the site. It offers three basic tools: TextBox, CheckBox, and RadioButton.

Use the TextBox control

This tool allows the user to enter text according to three styles determined by the value of the TextMode property:

SingleLine: Accept income as only one line.

MultiLine: Accept multiple-line access.

Password: The user's income appears as icons (stars *** or others).

ASP.net code

```
<div>
    <asp: TextBox ID = "TextBox1" runat = "server" TextMode = "SingleLine" />
    <asp: TextBox ID = "TextBox2" runat = "server" TextMode = "MultiLine" />
    <asp: TextBox ID = "TextBox3" runat = "server" TextMode = "Password" />
</div>
```

TextBox tool properties:

AccessKey: To select a key from the keyboard when pressed, the focus is moved to this tool.

AutoCompleteType: Specify an AutoComplete mode where a user needs to enter a few characters in order to show previously entered matching words. This property can be deactivated by assigning the Disabled value to it.

AutoPostBack: Send content to the server immediately when any changes in the entered text.

Columns: Specifies the number of columns that will appear.

Enabled: Activate or deactivate this tool.

MaxLength: Specifies the maximum number of characters that can be entered (do not work with MulitLine).

ReadOnly: Prevents the user from changing the value in the TextBox.

Rows: Specifies the number of lines that will appear.

TabIndex: Specifies a number indicating the order of access for this tool via the Tab key.

Warp: Specifies whether text can be automatically wrapped with MultiLine mode.

The TextBox control supports the Focus method that allows focus to be placed on execution, and supports the TextChanged event that is fired when the contents of this tool change.

To illustrate how the AutoPostBack property works, create a new page, add TextBox1 and set the previous property to True, then add Lable1. What we will do is that when you type text, it will be displayed in the Label1 tool once the focus is moved out of TextBox1. :

ASP.net code

```
  <div>

     <asp: TextBox ID = "TextBox1" runat = "server"
AutoPostBack = "True"

        ontextchanged = "TextBox1_TextChanged"> </ asp:
TextBox>
```

```
    <asp: Label ID = "Label1" runat = "server" Text =
"Label"> <asp: Label>
  </div>
```

In the TextChanged event of the TextBox1 tool, type the following code:

#C code

```
  protected void TextBox1_TextChanged (object sender,
EventArgs e)
  {
     Label1.Text = TextBox1.Text;
  }
```

VB code

```
  Protected Sub TextBox1_TextChanged (ByVal sender As
Object, ByVal e As
  System.EventArgs) Handles TextBox1.TextChanged

     Label1.Text = TextBox1.Text
```

End Sub

Execute the page, type what you want in TextBox1, press the Tab key on the keyboard and see the result, close the browser and then execute again and type the first letter of the value you entered in the first execution to see how the autocomplete process is done, deactivate the autocomplete feature as shown above Then retry and retype the same word to notice that AutoComplete has stopped.

Use the CheckBox control tool

This tool allows the user to decide whether to accept or reject an order, ie it is considered as a question to the user and the answer is inevitably either yes or no, e.g. Find out the user option as we'll see shortly.

Properties of the CheckBox control:

* AccessKey: To select a key from the keyboard when pressed, the focus is moved to this tool.

* AutoPostBack: Send the selection option to the server immediately in case of any change.

* Checked: Returns True or False depending on user acceptance or rejection.

* Enabled: Activate or deactivate this tool.

*TabIndex: Specifies a number indicating the order of access for this tool via the Tab key.

* Text: Select the text that appears next to this tool (question asked).

* TextAlign: The position of the text for the tool, to its right or left, takes one of the values Left, Right.

The CheckBox control supports the Focus method that allows focus to be placed on execution, and it triggers the CheckedChanged event when a user changes their choice whether to reject or accept.

A simple example: Create a new page with the tools CheckBox1, Button1, Label1 Click the Button1 button twice and type the following code:

#C code

protected void Button1_Click (object sender, EventArgs e)

```
{
   Label1.Text = CheckBox1.Checked.ToString ();
}
```

VB code

```
  Protected Sub Button1_Click1 (ByVal sender As Object,
ByVal e As
   System.EventArgs) Handles Button1.Click

     Label1.Text = CheckBox1.Checked.ToString ()
   End Sub
```

Execute and select the CheckBox option and then press the button, you will see that the Checked property has returned True, deactivate the option and press the button again. What is the result now?

Page code after making minor modifications to the properties as follows:

ASP.net code

```
<div>

      <asp: CheckBox ID = "CheckBox1" runat = "server"
Text = "Receive messages on mobile?"

                TextAlign = "Left" /> <br />

      <asp: Button ID = "Button1" runat = "server" Text =
"ok"

                onclick = "Button1_Click" /> <br />

      <asp: Label ID = "Label1" runat = "server" Text = "" />

  </div>
```

Note: The ASP.Net workstation supports the CheckBoxList tool, which allows you to make a list of its elements, CheckBox tools, as we will see in a later lesson.

Use the RadioButton control

This tool does not appear individually but is always within a group where the user can select only one option within a group's tools.

RadioButton Control Properties:

* AccessKey: To select a key from the keyboard when pressed, the focus is moved to this tool.

* AutoPostBack: Send the selection option to the server immediately in case of any change.

* Checked: Returns True or False depending on user acceptance or rejection.

* Enabled: Activate or deactivate this tool.

* GroupName: To join the RadioButton tool into a group, from each group only one option can be selected from the RadionButton tools in it.

* TabIndex: Specifies a number indicating the order of access for this tool via the Tab key.

* Text: Select the text that appears next to this tool (the option presented).

* TextAlign: The position of the text for the tool, to its right or left, takes one of the values Left, Right.

The RadioButton control supports the Focus method that allows focus to be placed on execution, and also triggers the CheckedChanged event when the user changes his option.

Here's a simple overview of how this tool works, create a new page and add the following tools: RadioButton 3, button, Label, modify the Text property of RadioButton tools so that each tool displays a specific color, and (very important) you should take the previous three tools Same as GroupName, we press the button twice and type the following code:

#C code

```
protected void Button1_Click (object sender, EventArgs e)
  {
     string color = "";
     if (RadioButton1.Checked)
        color = RadioButton1.Text;
     if (RadioButton2.Checked)
        color = RadioButton2.Text;
     if (RadioButton3.Checked)
        color = RadioButton3.Text;
     Label1.Text = "Your Favorite color is:" + color;
  }
```

VB code

```
Protected Sub Button1_Click (ByVal sender As Object, ByVal e As
System.EventArgs) Handles Button1.Click

    Dim color As String = ""
    If RadioButton1.Checked Then
        color = RadioButton1.Text
    End If
    If RadioButton2.Checked Then
        color = RadioButton2.Text
    End If
    If RadioButton3.Checked Then
        color = RadioButton3.Text
    End If
    Label1.Text = "Your Favorite color is:" + color
End Sub
```

The page code is as follows:

ASP.net code

```
<div>
Favorite color? <br />
    <asp: RadioButton ID = "RadioButton1" runat =
"server" Text = "Red"
        GroupName = "colors" /> <br />
    <asp: RadioButton ID = "RadioButton2" runat =
"server" Text = "Green"
        GroupName = "colors" /> <br />
    <asp: RadioButton ID = "RadioButton3" runat =
"server" Text = "Blue"
        GroupName = "colors" /> <br />
    <asp: Button ID = "Button1" runat = "server" Text =
"ok"
            onclick = "Button1_Click" />
    <br />
    <asp: Label ID = "Label1" runat = "server" Text = "" />
</div>
```

Delete the GroupName property from the previous code and execute and try to choose more than one color.

Note: The ASP.Net platform supports the RadioButtonList tool, which allows you to create a list of its elements, RadioButton tools, as we will see in a later lesson.

We have reached the end of the first lesson. In the next lesson, we will discuss how to send form data to the server with various button tools.

Chapter II

Submit form data

In the previous chapter, we introduced the basic controls that are built into the ASP.NET platform. In this chapter we will learn how to send form data to the server with various button tools.

The ASP.Net platform provides us with three tools to send form data to the server: Button, LinkButton and ImageButton. They perform the same functionality but each has its own appearance and features that distinguish it from others.

Use the Button control

When you click on this tool, it sends the page data to the server to be processed and the code within the Click event of this tool is executed. The following example shows the current time in the Label tool. Twice and type the following code:

#C code

```
protected void Button1_Click (object sender, EventArgs e)
  {
     Label1.Text = DateTime.Now.ToString ("T");
  }
```

VB code

```
Protected Sub Button1_Click (ByVal sender As Object,
ByVal e As
 System.EventArgs) Handles Button1.Click
   Label1.Text = DateTime.Now.ToString ("T")
End Sub
```

Full Code Page:

ASP.net code

```
  <div>
     <asp: Button ID = "Button1" runat = "server" Text =
"Button"
              onclick = "Button1_Click" />
     <br />
     <asp: Label ID = "Label1" runat = "server" Text = "" />
  </div>
```

Notice that when the button is pressed, the entire page is reloaded, sent to the server, processed and then returned to the user.

Button Control Properties

AccessKey: To select a key from the keyboard when pressed, the focus is moved to this tool.

CommandArgument: Specifies a variable that is sent to the Command event.

CommandName: Specifies the name of the command that is sent to the Command event.

Enabled: Activate or deactivate this tool.

OnClientClick: Specifies the code to be executed on the user's device when the button is pressed.

PostBackUrl: Move to a specific page after sending data to the server.

TabIndex: Specifies a number indicating the order of access for this tool via the Tab key.

Text: Select the text that appears on this tool.

UseSubmitBehavior: Enables us to use JavaScript to send form data.

The Button control supports the Focus method, which allows focus to be placed on execution, and supports two events:

Click: Launches when the button is pressed.

Command: Launches when the button is pressed, and CommandArgument and CommandName are passed to this event.

Use the LinkButton control

It does the same thing as the Button tool, but it differs in appearance. It looks like a link, not a button, so you can select a page to navigate through. Let's do the same example, but replace the Button tool with the LinkButton tool, the code that runs when LinkButton is pressed:

#C code

```
protected void LinkButton1_Click (object sender, EventArgs e)
{
    Label1.Text = DateTime.Now.ToString ("T");
}
```

VB code

```
   Protected Sub LinkButton1_Click (ByVal sender As
Object, ByVal e As

   System.EventArgs) Handles LinkButton1.Click


      Label1.Text = DateTime.Now.ToString ("T")

   End Sub
```

Page Code:

ASP.net code

```
   <div>

      <asp: LinkButton ID = "LinkButton1" runat = "server"

            onclick = "LinkButton1_Click"> LinkButton
</asp: LinkButton>

      <br />

      <asp: Label ID = "Label1" runat = "server" Text = "" />

   </div>
```

The LinkButton tool invisibly executes JavaScript code and specifically the doPostBack_ method which is responsible for sending data to the server. In our previous example, the code looks like this:

ASP.net code

```
<a id="LinkButton1" href="javascript:__doPostBack(
'LinkButton1' ,,'')"> Submit </a>
```

Properties of the LinkButton control

AccessKey: To select a key from the keyboard when pressed, the focus is moved to this tool.

CommandArgument: Specifies a variable that is sent to the Command event.

CommandName: Specifies the name of the command that is sent to the Command event.

Enabled: Activate or deactivate this tool.

OnClientClick: Specifies the code to execute on the user's device when this tool is clicked.

PostBackUrl: Move to a specific page after sending data to the server.

TabIndex: Specifies a number indicating the order of access for this tool via the Tab key.

Text: Select the text that appears on this tool.

The LinkButton control supports the Focus method that allows focus to be placed on execution and supports two events:

Click: Launches when this tool is pressed.

Command: Launches when you press the tool, and CommandArgument and CommandName are passed to this event.

Use the HyperLink control

This tool is the most common and simple way to navigate between different pages, unlike LinkButton, it does not send data to the server.

HyperLink Control Properties:

Enabled: Activate or deactivate this tool.

ImageUrl: Specifies the path and name of an image to be displayed as a link.

NavigateUrl: Specifies the URL to go to when this tool is clicked.

Text: Select the text that appears on this tool.

Target: enables us to open the link page in a new browser window.

Note: If values for Text and ImageUrl are specified together, then the image will be displayed because its priority is higher and the text specified in the Text property will not be displayed.

Example: Create a new page, add HyperLink and set its properties as follows:

ASP.net code

```
<div>
    <asp: HyperLink ID = "HyperLink1" runat = "server"
ImageUrl = "~ / images / img.png"
            NavigateUrl = "~ / Default14.aspx"> Go to
Page Defaul14 page
```

```
    </ asp: HyperLink>
  </div>
```

Execute the previous page and note that the Go to Page Defaul14 page text does not appear, only the selected image appears.

Use the ImageButton control

It performs the same function as the two previous tools, which send form data to the server and appear as an image on the web page, first to identify the characteristics of this tool and then apply an example.

ImageButton Control Properties:

AccessKey: To select a key from the keyboard when pressed, the focus is moved to this tool.

AlternateText: Alternate text that displays if the selected image is not displayed.

DescriptionUrl: Specifies a link to a page with details about the image.

CommandArgument: Specifies a variable that is sent to the Command event.

CommandName: Specifies the name of the command that is sent to the Command event.

Enabled: Activate or deactivate this tool.

ImageAlign: Locates the image for other html tools and can take one of the following values: AbsBottom, AbsMiddle, Baseline, Bottom, Left, Middle, NotSet, Right, TextTop, Top.

ImageUrl: Specifies the path and name of the image to be displayed.

OnClientClick: Specifies the code to execute on the user's device when this tool is clicked.

PostBackUrl: Move to a specific page after sending data to the server.

TabIndex: Specifies a number indicating the order of access for this tool via the Tab key.

The ImageButton control supports the Focus method that allows focus to be placed on execution and supports two events:

Click: Launches when this tool is pressed.

Command: Launches when you press the tool, and CommandArgument and CommandName are passed to this event.

Example: In the following example, we will determine the coordinates of where the user is pressed on the ImageButton tool.

Create a new page in which to place the ImageButton tool and make it display an image via the ImageUrl property and then add the Label tools, click on the ImageButton twice and type the following code:

#C code

```
protected void ImageButton1_Click (object sender,
ImageClickEventArgs e)
{
    Label1.Text = "X =" + e.X.ToString ();
    Label2.Text = "Y =" + e.Y.ToString ();
}
```

VB code

```
Protected Sub ImageButton1_Click (ByVal sender As
Object, ByVal e As
System.Web.UI.ImageClickEventArgs) Handles
ImageButton1.Click

    Label1.Text = "X =" + e.X.ToString ()
    Label2.Text = "Y =" + e.Y.ToString ()
End Sub
```

Page Code:

ASP.net code

```
<div>
    <asp: ImageButton ID = "ImageButton1" runat =
"server"
        ImageUrl = "~ / images / img.png"
        onclick = "ImageButton1_Click" />
    <br />
```

```
    <asp: Label ID = "Label1" runat = "server" Text = "" />
    <asp: Label ID = "Label2" runat = "server" Text = "" />
</div>
```

Note: When working with any tool that displays images, it is strongly recommended that we use the AlternateText feature to display alternative text. Some users cancel the option to display images in the browser in order to get faster browsing.

Send data across pages

By default, when a button is pressed on a page, it is sent to the server and the data is processed and then displayed on the same page, i.e., the page reloads with modified data. first.

Example: Create a new page called search.aspx Add TextBox and Button, give the PostBackUrl value results.aspx which is the second page we create, this property, as we saw earlier, makes the server redirects the browser to a specific page when you press the button, what we want from this example The user enters some text into the TextBox and then presses the button for the server to display the same text, but on another page, page code search.aspx:

ASP.net code

```
  <div>

    <asp: TextBox ID = "TxtSearch" runat = "server">
<asp: TextBox>

    <br />

    <asp: Button ID = "BtnSearch" runat = "server" Text =
"search"

            PostBackUrl = "~ / results.aspx" />

  </div>
```

Now we move to the results.aspx page and add only the Label tool to display the text entered on the first page where the code is as follows:

ASP.net code

```
  <div>
```

```
    <asp: Label ID = "LblSearch" runat = "server" Text = ""
/>
  </div>
```

In the page loading event we write the following code:

#C code

```
  protected void Page_Load (object sender, EventArgs e)
  {
    if (PreviousPage! = null)
    {
      TextBox txtSearch = (TextBox)
PreviousPage.FindControl ("TxtSearch");
      LblSearch.Text = String.Format ("Search for: {0}",
txtSearch.Text);
    }
  }
```

VB code

```
Protected Sub Page_Load (ByVal sender As Object,
ByVal e As System.EventArgs)
Handles Me.Load

    If PreviousPage IsNot Nothing Then
        Dim txtSearch As TextBox =
        DirectCast (PreviousPage.FindControl
("TxtSearch"), TextBox)
        LblSearch.Text = [String] .Format ("Search for: {0}",
txtSearch.Text)
    End If
End Sub
```

Analyze Previous Code: PreviousPage is used to get a pointer to the previous page that caused us to be moved to this page. The FindControl method returns a specific control and all its current properties (we want to retrieve the value of the Text property from it). search and enter some text and then press the button to see how the code and PostBackUrl function work and how we were able to access previous page data from the next page.

Note: There are more effective methods to transfer data between pages of the site such as Cookies, Session and others and we will discuss them in detail in later lessons, God willing.

Select the default button

This property allows you to select a button on the page so that the code inside it is executed by simply pressing the Enter key from the keyboard and without having to press the button with the mouse, this property is called defaultButton and is specified as a property of the form.

Example: Create a new page, add two Button tools and one Label tool. In the first button click event, type the following code:

#C code

```
protected void Button1_Click (object sender, EventArgs e)
{
    Label1.Text = "you click Button1";
}
```

VB code

```
   Protected Sub Button1_Click (ByVal sender As Object,
ByVal e As
   System.EventArgs) Handles Button1.Click

      Label1.Text = "you click Button1"
   End Sub
```

In the second button click event:

#C code

```
   protected void Button2_Click (object sender, EventArgs
e)
   {
      Label1.Text = "you click Button2";
   }
```

```
Protected Sub Button2_Click (ByVal sender As Object,
ByVal e As
System.EventArgs) Handles Button2.Click

    Label1.Text = "you click Button2"
End Sub
```

Now we come to the bottom line which is to specify the defaultButton property of the form and give it as the value of one of the two previous buttons as in the following code:

ASP.net code

```
<form id = "form1" runat = "server" defaultbutton =
"Button2">
<div>
    <asp: Button ID = "Button1" runat = "server" Text =
"Button"
            onclick = "Button1_Click" />
    <br />
```

```
<asp: Button ID = "Button2" runat = "server" Text =
"Button"
            onclick = "Button2_Click" />
    <br />
    <asp: Label ID = "Label1" runat = "server" Text = "">
<asp: Label>
  </div>
  </form>
```

Where Button2 is selected as the default button, execute the page and press Enter to see what happens. Repeat the example after modifying the previous property and making it equal to Button1.

Note: The defaultButton property can be used with the Panel control, which we will learn in detail in upcoming lessons.

Process the Command event

The Buttons of all three types support the Click and Command events as we saw earlier. The difference between these two events is that when working with Command we can pass a command name and a variable to the command as well. These things are not supported with the Click event.

Example: Create a new page, add two Button tools and one Label tool, add the Button tools onCommand, CommandName, CommandArgument

ASP.net code

```
   <div>
      <asp: Button ID = "Button1" runat = "server" Text =
"Red"
         oncommand = "Button_Command"
         CommandName = "colors"
         CommandArgument = "Red" />
      <asp: Button ID = "Button2" runat = "server" Text =
"Blue"
         oncommand = "Button_Command"
         CommandName = "colors"
         CommandArgument = "Blue" />
```

```
<asp: Label ID = "Label1" runat = "server" Text = "">
<asp: Label>
  </div>
```

We open the default.aspx.cs file and write the following code:

#C code

```
  protected void Button_Command (object sender,
CommandEventArgs e)
  {
    if (e.CommandName == "colors")
    {
      switch (e.CommandArgument.ToString ())
      {
        case "Red":
          Label1.Text = "RED";
          break;
        case "Blue":
```

```
            Label1.Text = "BLUE";
            break;
        }
    }
}
```

VB code

```
Protected Sub Button_Command (ByVal sender As
Object, ByVal e As
CommandEventArgs)

If e.CommandName = "colors" Then
    Select Case e.CommandArgument.ToString ()
        Case "Red"
            Label1.Text = "RED"
        Exit Select
        Case "Blue"
            Label1.Text = "BLUE"
        Exit Select
```

```
    End Select
  End If
  End Sub
```

Note that both buttons call the same code Button_Commaen with CommandName set to colors and the only difference between them is the scroll variable where the first button sends the Red variable while the second button sends the blue variable, execute the page to see the result of the action. A set of buttons with the same code, but with different variables, saving us the trouble of rewriting the code if the Click event were used.

In this lesson, we have identified three tools for sending form data to the server: Button, LinkButton, and ImageButton with examples for each. In the next lesson, we will introduce two new tools for displaying images in ASP.NET.

Chapter III

View images

In the previous lesson, we learned how to send form data to the server with various button tools. In this lesson, we will introduce two tools for displaying images in ASP.NET.

The ASP.NET platform offers two image rendering tools: Image and ImageMap. The Image Control tool displays images in a simple way, while the ImageMap tool offers more complex features. We'll learn about both tools in the following paragraphs.

Use the Image control

Using the Image control to display a specific image through the ImageUrl property, we will learn some of the properties of this tool and then apply an example.

Image Control Properties:

AlternateText: Alternate text that displays if the selected image is not displayed.

DescriptionUrl: Specifies a link to a page with details about the image.

GenerateEmptyAlternateText: Assign an empty string as alternate text for the image.

ImageAlign: Locates the image for other html tools and can take one of the following values: AbsBottom, AbsMiddle, Baseline, Bottom, Left, Middle, NotSet, Right, TextTop, Top.

ImageUrl: Specifies the path and name of the image to be displayed.

Example: In the following example we will make the Image tool display one of three images and randomly, create a new page and add the Image Tool, create within the project a new folder named images Add three images and be named pic1, pic2, pic3 Open the code file back any page Default.aspx.cs In the Page Load event (Page_Load), type the following code:

#C code

```
protected void Page_Load (object sender, EventArgs e)
```

```
{
   Random rnd = new Random ();
   switch (rnd.Next (3))
   {
      case 0:
         Image1.ImageUrl = "~ / images / pic1.png";
         Image1.AlternateText = "picture1";
         break;
      case 1:
         Image1.ImageUrl = "~ / images / pic2.png";
         Image1.AlternateText = "picture2";
         break;
      case 2:
         Image1.ImageUrl = "~ / images / pic3.png";
         Image1.AlternateText = "picture3";
         break;
   }
}
```

VB code

```
  Protected Sub Page_Load (ByVal sender As Object,
ByVal e As EventArgs)
   Handles Me.Load

   Dim rnd As New Random ()
   [Next] (3)
      Case 0
         Image1.ImageUrl = "~ / images / pic1.bmp"
         Image1.AlternateText = "picture1"
      Exit Select
      Case 1
         Image1.ImageUrl = "~ / images / pic2.jpg"
         Image1.AlternateText = "picture2"
      Exit Select
      Case 2
         Image1.ImageUrl = "~ / images / pic3.bmp"
         Image1.AlternateText = "picture3"
      Exit Select
```

```
    End Select
End Sub
```

Execute the previous page To display one of the three images, press the Refresh Page button (or F5) to display another image randomly. In the following paragraph we will learn about a tool that is also used to display images but with more varied options and features.

Use the ImageMap control tool

This tool is used to display an image as well as to associate it with an invisible map.In other words, when the user clicks on different parts of the image, we can also respond to different reactions depending on the coordinates of the location of the click on the image.As such, we can use this tool as a way to navigate between pages, for example. Where we display an image containing graphics expressing the following pages and then determine when clicking on a site from this image page to be moved, another use of this tool is to determine the user's income where we can display an image containing several products and the option of the user depending on the product Pressure Les on the image.

The ImageMap control is automatically associated with the HotSpot class, which allows you to select clickable areas on the ImageMap tool.

CircleHotSpot: Enables us to define a circular area on the image map.

PolygonHotSpot: Enables us to define an irregular shape on the map image.

RectangleHotSpot: Enables us to select a rectangular area on the map image.

ImageMap Control Properties:

AccessKey: To select a key from the keyboard when pressed, the focus is moved to this tool.

AlternateText: Alternate text that displays if the selected image is not displayed.

DescriptionUrl: Specifies a link to a page with details about the image.

GenerateEmptyAlternateText: Assign an empty string as alternate text for the image.

HotSpotMode: Specifies the behavior that will be performed when you press an area of the image and take one of the following values: Inactive, Navigate, NotSet, PostBack.

HotSpots: Enables you to get all the HotSpots within the ImageMap control.

ImageAlign: Locates the image for other html tools and can take one of the following values: AbsBottom, AbsMiddle, Baseline, Bottom, Left, Middle, NotSet, Right, TextTop, Top.

ImageUrl: Specifies the path and name of the image to be displayed.

TabIndex: Specifies a number indicating the order of access for this tool via the Tab key.

Target: Allows us to open the page in a new window....

The ImageMap control supports the Focus method that allows focus to be placed on execution. It supports the Click event that is fired when an area of this tool is pressed and the HotSpotMode property takes the PostBack value.

Example: In the example, we will show you how to use one aspect of the ImageMap control, where we will create a menu to navigate between different pages, create a new project and add four pages to be named Dafault, page1, page2, page3. Add on the Default ImageMap page and have it display an image that is appropriate for the previous purpose.

Where we will divide the previous image tool into three areas and each region takes us to a specific page.

Default.aspx page code:

ASP.net code

```
<div>
    <asp: ImageMap ID = "ImageMap1" runat = "server"
            ImageUrl = "~ / images / navigationBar.jpg">

    <asp: RectangleHotSpot NavigateUrl = "~ /
page1.aspx" Left = "0" Top = "0"
        Right = "100" Bottom = "30" AlternateText = "go
to page1" />

    <asp: RectangleHotSpot NavigateUrl = "~ /
page2.aspx" Left = "100" Top = "0"
```

```
Right = "200" Bottom = "30" AlternateText = "go
to page2" />


<asp: RectangleHotSpot NavigateUrl = "~ /
page3.aspx" Left = "200" Top = "0"

Right = "300" Bottom = "30" AlternateText = "go
to page3" />


</ asp: ImageMap>

</div>
```

Note from the preceding code that the RectangleHotSpot property has sub-properties Left, Right, Top, Bottom to determine the coordinates of the region (image size in example 300x30). Each region is linked to a specific page via the NavigateUrl property to be moved to the browser when you click that area.

Another example: Now that we have learned how to use the ImageMap tool to navigate between different pages, we will show here how to work with PostBack ie stay within the same page, add a new page and add TextBox and ImageMap, the desired image to be displayed.

What is required is that when you press the first region (ToUpper), the text in the TextBox tool is converted to uppercase, and when the second region (ToLower) is pressed, the text in the TextBox tool is converted to lower case, and pressing the third area clears (Erase) Text found in the TextBox tool, click the ImageMap tool twice and add the following code:

#C code

```
protected void ImageMap1_Click (object sender,
ImageMapEventArgs e)
{
    switch (e.PostBackValue)
    {
        case "ToUpper":
            TextBox1.Text = TextBox1.Text.ToUpper ();
            break;
        case "ToLower":
            TextBox1.Text = TextBox1.Text.ToLower ();
            break;
        case "Erase":
```

```
        TextBox1.Text = String.Empty;
        break;
    }
}
```

VB code

```
Select Case e.PostBackValue
    Case "ToUpper"
        TextBox1.Text = TextBox1.Text.ToUpper ()
    Exit Select
    Case "ToLower"
        TextBox1.Text = TextBox1.Text.ToLower ()
    Exit Select
    Case "Erase"
        TextBox1.Text = [String] .Empty
    Exit Select
End Select
```

In the previous code we received the PostBackVlaue property, whose value is determined by the area being pressed in the ImageMap tool as we will see, page code:

ASP.net code

```
<div>

    <asp: ImageMap ID = "ImageMap1" runat = "server"
HotSpotMode = "PostBack"
        ImageUrl = "~ / images / textCase.jpg" onclick =
"ImageMap1_Click">

    <asp: RectangleHotSpot PostBackValue = "ToUpper"
Left = "0" Top = "0" Right = "100"
                    Bottom = "30" AlternateText =
"ToUpper" />

    <asp: RectangleHotSpot PostBackValue = "ToLower"
Left = "100" Top = "0"
                    Right = "200" Bottom = "30"
AlternateText = "ToLower" />
```

```
<asp: RectangleHotSpot PostBackValue = "Erase" Left = "200" Top = "0" Right = "300"
                    Bottom = "30" AlternateText = "Erase" />
    </ asp: ImageMap>

    <br />

    <asp: TextBox ID = "TextBox1" runat = "server" TextMode = "MultiLine" />

  </div>
```

In the preceding code, the HotSpotMode property is set to the PostBack value.

Use the Panel control

This tool enables us to work with the ASP.Net toolkit at once. A behavior is applied to all controls within the Panel tool. For example, if this control is hidden, all the tools within it will disappear and if the Panel tool is deactivated. All controls within it and so on will be deactivated.

Panel Control Features:

DefaultButton: This feature enables us to select a default button within the Panel tool that searches the code inside it once the Enter key is pressed from the keyboard.

Direction: Determine the orientation of text and tools within Panel You can take one of the following values NotSet, LeftToRight, RightToLeft.

GroupingText: Specifies a title for the Panel tool.

HorizontalAlign: Specifies the horizontal alignment of the contents of the Panel tool and can take one of the following values NotSet, Justify, Left, Center, Right.

ScrollBars: Shows a horizontal or vertical scroll bar (or both) for the Panel tool and takes one of the following values None, Horizontal, Vertical, Both, Auto.

Example: In the following application we will add a panel and then add a set of different controls to see that the application of something to the panel will be applied to the...

Example: In the following application we will add a panel and then add a set of different controls to see that the application of a command on the panel will be applied to the tools inside them as well, create a new page, add a control panel and put a group of controls and then put one button Outside the page code should look like this:

ASP.net code

```
<div>

<asp: Panel id = "pnlContact" GroupingText = "Contact
Information" Runat = "server">
    <asp: Label id = "lblFirstName" Text = "First Name:"
            AssociatedControlID = "txtFirstName" Runat =
"server" />
    <br />
```

```
        <asp: TextBox id = "txtFirstName" AutoCompleteType
= "FirstName" Runat = "server"

                />

        <br /> <br />

        <asp: Label id = "lblLastname" Text = "Last Name:"

                AssociatedControlID = "txtLastName" Runat =
"server" />

        <br />

        <asp: TextBox id = "txtLastName" AutoCompleteType
= "LastName" Runat = "server"

                />

        <br /> <br />

        <asp: Button id = "btnSubmit" Text = "Submit" Runat
= "server" />

    </ asp: Panel>


    <br />

    <asp: Button ID = "Button1" runat = "server" Text =
"Visible" onclick = "Button1_Click"

            />

    </div>
```

The code that is added to the Button1 event is:

#C code

```
   protected void Button1_Click (object sender, EventArgs
e)
   {
      pnlContact.Visible =! pnlContact.Visible;
   }
```

VB code

```
   Protected Sub Button1_Click (ByVal sender As Object,
ByVal e As EventArgs)
      pnlContact.Visible = Not pnlContact.Visible
   End Sub
```

Run the previous application to see the effect of the Panel properties on its contents.

If the Panel control groups controls with a common function or attributes determined by the method of work into groups, for the purpose of organizing the page and taking advantage of the benefits offered by this tool.

Chapter IV

Upload files to the site

In the previous lessons we have studied the standard tools that should be used in most ASP.Net applications. In the next tutorials, we will discuss more specialized controls, known as Rich controls.

In this lesson you will learn how to allow browsers to upload files on the site, such as uploading pictures, videos, etc.

Upload files to the site

We use the FileUpload control tool to upload files to the site.

Properties of the FileUpload control

Enabled: Activate or deactivate this tool.

FileBytes: Get the contents of the file as a byte array.

FileContent: Gets the contents of the file as a stream.

FileName: Get the file name.

HasFile: Returns True when the file is uploaded.

PostedFile: Returns the uploaded file encapsulated for the purpose of the HttpPostedFile row.

The FileUpload control also supports the following methods:

Focus: Allows placing the focus on this tool.

SaveAs: Stores the file (to be uploaded) on the site.

The PostedFile property encapsulates the uploaded file for the purpose of HttpPostedFile. This allows additional information about the file.

The properties of the HttpPostedFile row

ContentLenght: Determines the file size in bytes.

ContentType: to see the file type (suffix).

FileName: to see the file name.

InputStream: Get the file as a stream.

The HttpPostedFile row also supports the SaveAs method, which stores the file on the site.

Note that the HttpPostedFile row introduces some of the properties previously provided with the FileUpload control that can be handled without the need for the HttpPostedFile row, for example to obtain the file name, you can use one of two methods:

FileUpload.FileName

HttpPostedFile.FileName

The SaveAs method is also present in the HttpPostedFile row even though it is explicitly available with the FileUpload control.

Example:

Create a new page and add the tools FileUpload1, Button1, Label1. Create a new folder inside the site files named uploads to upload files to it, in the event of the button press type the following code:

#C code

```
protected void Button1_Click (object sender, EventArgs e)
{
    try
    {
        if (FileUpload1.HasFile)
        {
            string path = "~ / uploads /" + FileUpload1.FileName;
            FileUpload1.SaveAs (MapPath (path));
            Label1.Text = "File Uploaded successfuly ...";
        }
    }
    catch (Exception ex) {}
}
```

VB code

```
   Protected Sub Button1_Click (ByVal sender As Object, 
ByVal e As
   System.EventArgs) Handles Button1.Click

      If (FileUpload1.HasFile) Then
         Dim filePath As String = "~ / uploads /" & 
FileUpload1.FileName
         FileUpload1.SaveAs (MapPath (filePath))
      End If
   End Sub
```

The page code should be as follows:

ASP.net code

```
   <div>
      <asp: FileUpload ID = "FileUpload1" runat = "server" 
/>
```

```
<br />
<asp: Button ID = "Button1" runat = "server" Text =
"Upload"
        onclick = "Button1_Click" />
<br />
<asp: Label ID = "Label1" runat = "server" Text = "" />
</div>
```

Execute the previous application and try to upload a file (eg image), close the execution. The file must have been added to the Upload folder. If you don't see it, click Update Site Files as follows:

image00_ (1) .thumb.png.03813da3f3bdcb089f

In the previous example, the user can upload any type of file, in the following example we will determine the patterns that we allow the user to upload (only some types of images).

Example:

Create a new page and add the tools FileUpload1, Button1, Label1. Create a new folder within the site files named uploads to upload files to it. In the push button event type the following code:

#C code

```
protected void Button1_Click (object sender, EventArgs
e)
{
    try
    {
        if (FileUpload1.HasFile)
        {
            if (CheckFileType (FileUpload1.FileName))
            {
                string path = "~ / uploads /" +
FileUpload1.FileName;
                FileUpload1.SaveAs (MapPath (path));
                Label1.Text = "File Uploaded successfuly ...";
            }
        }
```

```
    }
    catch (Exception ex) {}
  }
```

VB code

```
  Protected Sub Button1_Click (ByVal sender As Object, ByVal e As
  System.EventArgs) Handles Button1.Click

    If (FileUpload1.HasFile) Then
      If (CheckFileType (FileUpload1.FileName)) Then
        Dim filePath As String = "~ / uploads /" & FileUpload1.FileName
        FileUpload1.SaveAs (MapPath (filePath))
      End If
    End If
  End Sub
```

Call the IO namespace, where we add the following code at the top of the page:

#C code

```
using System.IO;
```

VB code

```
Imports System.IO
```

CheckFileType is responsible for checking the file type:

#C code

```
bool CheckFileType (string fileName)
{
    string ext = Path.GetExtension (fileName);
    switch (ext.ToLower ())
    {
        case ".gif":
            return true;
```

```
        case ".png":
          return true;
        case ".jpg":
          return true;
        case ".jpeg":
          return true;
        default:
          return false;
      }
    }
```

VB code

```
  Function CheckFileType (ByVal fileName As String) As
Boolean
    Dim ext As String = Path.GetExtension (fileName)
    Select Case ext.ToLower ()
      Case ".gif"
        Return True
      Case ".png"
```

```
        Return True
      Case ".jpg"
        Return True
      Case ".jpeg"
        Return True
      Case Else
        Return False
    End Select
  End Function
```

Previous Page Code:

ASP.net code

```
  <div>
    <asp: FileUpload ID = "FileUpload1" runat = "server"
/>
    <br />
    <asp: Button ID = "Button1" runat = "server" Text =
"Upload"
          onclick = "Button1_Click" />
```

```
    <br />
    <asp: Label ID = "Label1" runat = "server" Text = "" />
  </div>
```

Execute the previous application and try to upload a file that is different from the selected types, you will notice that the file is not uploaded, repeat the experiment with one of the previous image types to see the acceptance of the upload.

Upload files to a database

Since we store files in a database instead of a regular folder, this method causes enormous size of the database and therefore difficult and slow to transfer and deal with, and we need to convert files to binary data (0,1) in order to be stored in the table, the best and followed method In sites is to upload files to a normal folder and store the names of files uploaded within the database with the storage of other information about them, such as the date of upload. In general, we will not go into these details now, since we did not touch on the subject of databases, we will have a return to discuss how to upload files professionally in advanced lessons.

Note: Uploading files with sizes smaller than 4 MB is accepted (count to the first example and try uploading a file larger than this size to see that the process is not accepted) .To change the maximum size allowed for each file, open the Web.config file and add the fourth line code:

XML code

```
<configuration>
<system.web>
<compilation debug = "true" targetFramework = "4.0" />
        <httpRuntime maxRequestLength = "10240" />
</system.web>
</configuration>
```

The maximum size is set at 10240 KB (10 MB).

CPSIA information can be obtained
at www.ICGtesting.com
Printed in the USA
LVHW050519210122
708983LV00017B/1913